Making Difficult Words Easy

Code Reader Books provide codes with "sound keys" to help read difficult words. For example, a word that may be difficult to read is "unicorn," so it might be followed by a code like this: unicorn *(YOO-nih-korn)*. By providing codes with phonetic sound keys, Code Reader Books make reading easier and more enjoyable.

Examples of Code Reader™ Keys

Long a sound (as in make):
a *(with a silent e)* or **ay**
Examples: able *(AY-bul)*; break *(brake)*

Short i sound (as in sit): **i** or **ih**
Examples: myth *(mith)*; mission *(MIH-shun)*

Long i sound (as in by):
i *(with a silent e)* or **y**
Examples: might *(mite)*; bicycle *(BY-sih-kul)*

Keys for the long o sound (as in hope):
o *(with a silent e)* or **oh**
Examples: molten *(MOLE-ten)*; ocean *(OH-shen)*

Codes use dashes between syllables *(SIH-luh-buls)*, **and stressed syllables have capital letters.**

To see more Code Reader sound keys, see page 44.

Wild Baby Animals
A Code Reader™ Book
Green Series

This book, along with images and text, is published under license from The Creative Company. Originally published by as Baby Hippos, Baby Tigers, and Baby Gorillas © 2020 and 2019 Black Rabbit Books

Additions and revisions to text in this
licensed edition: Copyright © 2025 Treasure Bay, Inc.

All rights reserved.

Reading Consultant: Jennifer L. VanSlander, Ph.D., Asst. Professor of Educational Leadership, Columbus State University

Code Reader™ is a trademark of Treasure Bay, Inc.

Patent Pending.
Code Reader books are designed using an innovative system of methods to create and include phonetic codes to enhance the readability of text. Reserved rights include any patent rights.

Published by
Treasure Bay, Inc.
PO Box 519
Roseville, CA 95661 USA

Printed in China

Library of Congress Control Number: 2024944963

ISBN: 978-1-60115-731-7

Visit us online at:
CodeReader.org

PR-1-25

Contents

CHAPTER 1
Baby Tigers 2

CHAPTER 2
Baby Gorillas 16

CHAPTER 3
Baby Hippos 28

Glossary 42

Questions to
Think About 43

Sound Keys for Codes 44

CHAPTER 1

A deer munches on some leaves. Nearby, a mother tiger and her cubs hide. The mother stands still, waiting for the perfect moment *(MOH-ment)* to pounce *(powns)*. Suddenly, the cubs leap and the startled *(STAR-tuld)* deer runs away! The playful cubs have made Mom miss her chance to catch dinner. But she is not upset. She simply sits down to rest and wait for another deer.

Meanwhile *(MEEN-wile)*, the cubs chase and swat *(swot)* each other. In time, they will be serious *(SEE-ree-us)* hunters. But for now, they're just two very small and wild *(WYuld)* baby tigers.

Tigers don't roar often, but when they do, it can be heard *(hurd)* for over a mile!

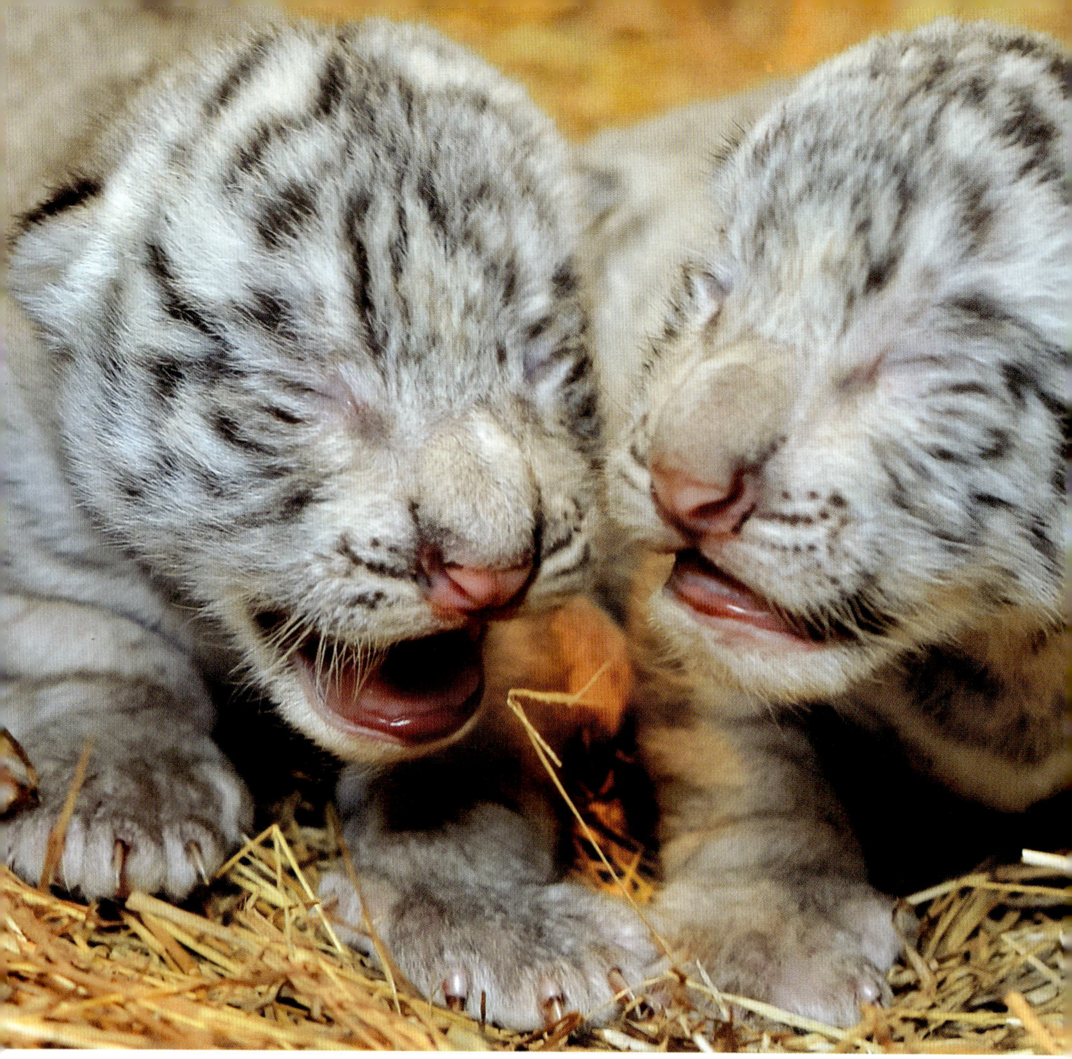

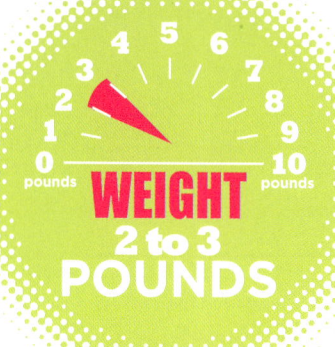

0 pounds
1
2
3
4
5
6
7
8
9
10 pounds
WEIGHT
2 to 3
POUNDS

How Much Does a Newborn Cub Weigh *(way)*?

Tigers are the largest cat species *(SPEE-sheez)* on the planet. They can be six to ten feet long, and they can weigh *(way)* anywhere from 220 to 660 pounds. Kittens weigh only about two to three pounds when they are born, so they have a lot of growing *(GROH-wing)* to do!

Tigers are powerful hunters, but they start off as helpless cubs. They are blind *(BLYnd)*, toothless, and wobbly. They need their mothers to protect and care for them. About one to two weeks after birth, cubs' eyes open and they get their first teeth. They totter around as they learn *(lurn)* to walk. As they grow stronger, they pounce and play with other cubs. It looks like they are having fun, but they are actually *(AK-choo-uh-lee)* practicing *(PRAK-tis-sing)* important skills for hunting.

Permanent teeth later replace the cubs' baby teeth.

Cubs start drinking their mothers' milk after birth *(burth)*, but that soon changes *(CHAYN-jez)*. At about six to eight weeks old, cubs start solid foods. Their mothers bring them meat from deer and wild pigs. By six months old, cubs only eat meat.

Tigers are apex *(AY-pex)* predators *(PRED-uh-turz)*, and mostly hunt large mammals *(MAM-ulz)* like deer and wild boar. They hunt primarily *(pry-MARE-uh-lee)* by sight and sound rather than by smell, and they typically *(TIP-ik-lee)* hunt alone.

An adult tiger can eat more than 50 pounds of food at one time.

From an early *(UR-lee)* age, cubs play at hunting with each other. They sneak, pounce, and pretend to bite. They learn these hunting skills by watching their mothers. At first, cubs just study and copy mom. Later, they will join in the hunt with her and, by 18 months *(munths)* old, the cubs can hunt on their own.

Killing Teeth

Tigers' teeth can be up to 3 inches long!

Tiger habitats—the places they live—include *(in-KLOOD)* forests, swamps, and grasslands. Adult tigers are solitary *(SOL-uh-tare-ee)* animals, often staying away from each other.

Each tiger has its own territory *(TAIR-uh-tor-ree)*, which is marked by spraying urine *(YUR-in)*, scratching trees, rubbing the scent *(sent)* from their cheeks on plants, and roaring.

TIGER RANGE MAP

Tiger habitats stretch from India *(IN-dee-uh)* to southeast China *(CHY-nuh)* and from the Russian *(RUSH-in)* Far East to Sumatra *(soo-MAH-truh)*, a large island *(i-lend)* in Indonesia *(in-doh-NEE-zjuh)*.

Tigers have been known to live up to 20 years of age *(aje)* in the wild. But on average *(AV-er-ij-rij)*, tigers live only 10 to 15 years.

Female *(FEE-male)* tigers give birth in hidden dens. They often have two to three cubs. For about two months, the cubs stay in the dens with Mom. Mother tigers protect their cubs and will fight off any predators *(PRED-uh-turz)*, which may include hyenas *(hy-EE-nuhz)*, crocodiles *(KROK-uh-dy-ulz)*, snakes, and even male tigers.

A mother tiger may call to its cubs with a roar. This will usually *(YOO-zhoo-uh-lee)* bring the cubs back in a hurry!

Cubs live with their mothers until they're about two years old. Then they leave to find their own territories *(TAIR-uh-TOR-reez)*. They explore and look for a good place to live. Some tigers move far away while others find a territory close to their mothers.

COMPARING SIZES

NEWBORN — about 2 to 3 POUNDS

SIX-MONTH-OLD — about 100 POUNDS

ADULT — up to 660 POUNDS

Young *(yung)* tigers grow bigger and stronger every day. At three to five years old, they're ready *(RED-ee)* to have their own cubs. But before then, there's much exploring *(ex-PLOR-ring)* to do!

Tigers like water. They are good swimmers.

CHAPTER 2

A baby hippopotamus *(hip-po-POT-uh-mus)* sinks beneath the surface *(SUR-fus)* of the water *(WAH-tur)*. It sits by its mother on the river bottom. The baby, called a calf *(kaf)*, checks out the underwater world. It sees rocks, reeds, and its family's great *(grate)* big feet. Soon, it's time to breathe *(breeth)* and the little hippo must get up to the surface *(SUR-fus)*. The calf pushes off a nearby rock and its mother gives it a boost. The calf takes a deep breath *(breth)*. Ahh!

Calves *(kavz)* spend a lot of time in water. In fact, female hippos often give birth in the water. The mothers guide *(gide)* their newborns to the surface, where the little hippos take their first big breaths *(breths)*.

Right after birth, mothers keep their newborns away from other hippos. This separation *(sep-uh-RAY-shun)* lets the babies and their mothers bond as the mothers lick and nuzzle their calves.

Hippo mothers do not leave their babies' sides for days, not even to eat. Instead *(in-STED)*, they remain in the water to watch over their calves *(kavz)* and to keep them safe from predators *(PRED-uh-turz)*. While adult hippos have few enemies, young hippos are at risk from lions *(LY-unz)*, hyenas *(hy-EE-nuhz)*, and crocodiles. With their powerful jaws and sharp teeth, adult hippos are fierce *(FEERes)* fighters, and the predators rarely win in a battle with Mom.

Hippos live in lakes and rivers in Africa *(AF-rih-kuh)*. They live in groups *(groops)* called pods. The pods often have 10 to 30 hippos, but some pods can have hundreds of members. One strong male, called a bull, usually *(YOO-zhoo-uh-lee)* leads each pod.

About two weeks after birth, mothers bring their calves into the pod. Pods can be dangerous *(DANE-jur-us)* places *(PLAY-sez)* for little hippos. Adult hippos sometimes fight. Calves could easily *(EE-zuh-lee)* be bitten, crushed, or killed if they're in the way.

Pods of hippos are also called bloats or sieges *(SEE-juz)*.

When the sun sets and the heat dies *(DYz)* down, adult hippos head out of the water to find food. They typically *(TIP-ik-lee)* feed on grass near the water but sometimes need to travel several miles to find food.

Very young calves will stay in the water and only drink their mother's milk. But when they are around four months old, they leave the water and go with the adults to try nibbling on plants. Mama cows knock and nip at their calves if they stray too far from them while grazing.

Adult hippos graze about six hours every night. They eat about 88 pounds of food at a time.

Hippos grow a lot in their first year. By about eight months old, they will no longer drink milk and will eat only plants. But even then, they don't go far from their mothers. Calves are not truly independent *(in-dee-PEN-dent)* until they are five to seven years old. By this time, they have grown from about 100 pounds at birth to about 3,000 pounds—the weight of a car!

HIPPO RANGE MAP

 Like many wild animals, hippos are suffering from habitat loss. However, they are still abundant *(uh-BUN-dent)* in many parts of East Africa.

 Hippos are one of the largest mammals *(MAM-mulz)* on Earth and can live to be about 40 years old in the wild.

Pods usually *(YOO-zhoo-uh-lee)* stay in water for 16 to 18 hours each day. Sometimes they relax near riverbanks. Hippo skin dries *(DRYz)* out in the heat and will crack if it gets too dry. Though *(thoh)* they spend much of their time in the water, surprisingly *(sur-PRIZE-zing-lee)*, hippos can't swim! Instead, they run underwater on the bottom of the river or lake. If they need to take a breath, they can push off the bottom to come to the surface of the water.

A two-month-old hippo can stay underwater for about 40 seconds before it needs to come up to breathe. An adult hippo comes up every three to five minutes to take a breath—and they can do this even while sleeping underwater!

Hippo skin makes red, oily "sunscreen." It protects the skin.

Young hippos like to play. They bob like dolphins *(DOL-finz)* in the water, chase each other, and have pushing contests! They stay mostly in shallow water where they prance along the river bottom. In deeper water, they ride on their mothers' backs.

When the young hippos become adults, the males will usually leave their pods. The females might stay and have their own babies. But until then, they have a lot of growing to do!

CHAPTER 3

Two young gorillas *(guh-RIL-uz)* wrestle *(REH-sul)* on the jungle floor. The small, black fuzz balls tumble and roll. They chase each other around tall trees. Using *(YOO-zing)* strong arms, they climb *(klime)* up the branches. The two look out from the leafy trees with bright eyes. What a big green world it is!

Baby gorillas are cute *(kyoot)* and playful. But babies aren't ready to play right away. First, they must spend months at their mothers' sides.

Mother gorillas hold their tiny *(TY-nee)* babies to their chests and the little gorillas hang on tight. Mothers also carry their little ones on their backs.

WEIGHT 4 to 5 POUNDS

How Much Does a New-born Gorilla Weigh?

At about two months old, baby gorillas start crawling *(KRAW-ling)* along the forest floor. At six to eight months old, they begin walking. Now they can walk behind their mothers, following them for short distances. But they will continue *(kun-TIN-yoo)* to ride on Mom's back when traveling far and will continue to ride until they're about three years old.

COMPARING WEIGHTS

NEWBORN
4 to 5 POUNDS

ADULT FEMALE
150 to 200 POUNDS

ADULT MALE
300 to 500 POUNDS

GORILLA RANGE MAP

Gorillas live in Africa's forests. Gorillas tend to live 35 to 40 years in the wild.

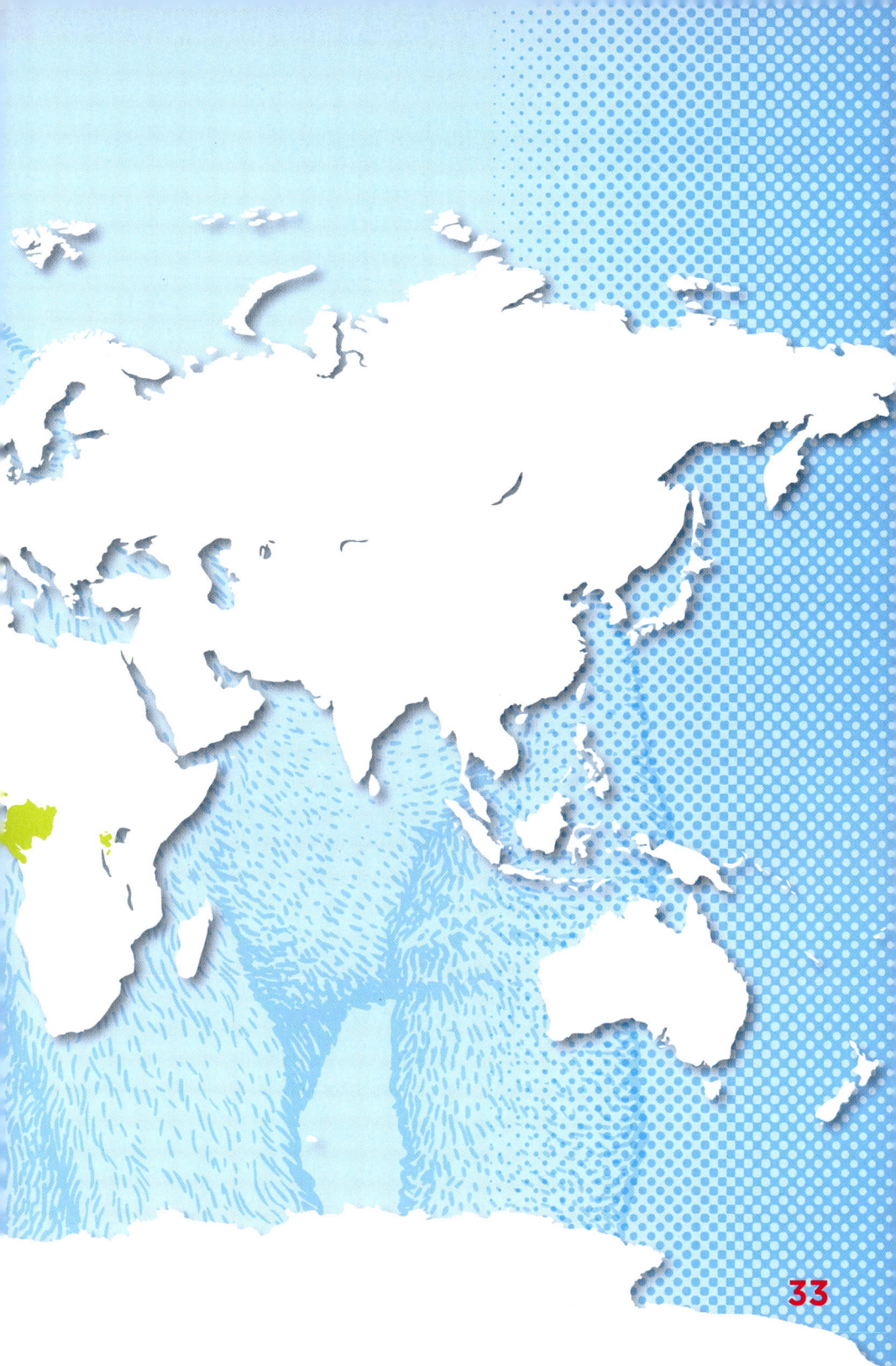

Gorillas sleep, eat, and play in groups *(groops)* called troops, which can have anywhere from five to thirty gorillas. A strong male, called a silverback, leads each troop.

Troops travel often and it is the silverback who decides where they eat and sleep. This leader will make sure the troop is safe and well-fed.

Silverbacks get their name from the silver hair on their backs.

Gorillas never use the same nest twice.

When not eating or playing, gorillas sleep and rest in nests. Smaller gorillas can nest in trees. Heavier *(HEV-ee-ur)* gorillas nest on the ground. Gorillas make their nests from leaves and branches. Mother gorillas share their nests with their young.

Baby gorillas are born toothless, so they can't eat solid *(SAH-lid)* food and can only drink their mothers' milk. At about six months old, the teeth appear *(uh-PEER)* and they begin trying solid foods. Fruit *(froot)* and bamboo quickly become some of a young gorilla's favorite *(FAY-voh-rit)* meals. Gorillas enjoy thistles *(THIS-ulz)* and insects too. But young gorillas won't eat solid food exclusively *(ex-KLOO-siv-lee)* until they are about three years old.

Gorillas eat many different things.

thistles fruit insects

bamboo bark

Adult male gorillas can eat up to 45 pounds of food each day.

After about three years riding on their mothers' backs, gorillas are finally *(FY-nuh-lee)* fully independent *(in-dee-PEND-ent)*. They quit drinking milk, eat only solid foods, and will make and sleep in their own nest.

Young gorillas learn by watching adults. They also learn by playing. Adults wrestle *(REH-sul)* with them. Young gorillas play-fight and chase each other. These actions *(AK-shunz)* let them practice *(PRAK-tis)* physical *(FIZ-uh-kul)* skills. They also help them form relationships *(ree-LAY-shun-ships)* with the other gorillas in the troop.

Just like humans *(HYOO-munz)*, gorillas form strong bonds with some members of the group. And, also like humans, they must learn to get along with everyone in the troop in order to keep things peaceful *(PEES-ful)*.

At about eight years old, a young gorilla will leave the troop. Some females find new groups to join. Or they may find males to start their own troops with. Males often live alone for a while. But while they are young, there's a lot of learning *(LUR-ning)* to do!

Gorillas touch *(tuch)* noses *(NOH-zez)* when greeting each other.

There are two gorilla species *(SPEE-sheez)* in the world: the eastern gorilla and the western gorilla. The mountain *(MOWN-tun)* gorilla is a subspecies *(SUB-spee-sheez)* of the eastern gorilla. Mountain gorillas are endangered *(en-DANE-jurd)*. There are estimated *(ES-tuh-tih-may-ted)* to be only a little over one thousand left in the wild.

Tigers are also classified as endangered. There are estimated to be less than five thousand in the wild.

Hippos are not yet classified *(KLAS-ih-fide)* as endangered, but their numbers have significantly *(sig-NIF-ih-kent-lee)* decreased *(dee-KREEST)* as their habitat has been reduced *(ree-DOOST)* due to human activity.

Many people are working very hard to preserve *(pree-ZURV)* spaces for these amazing *(uh-MAY-zing)* animals to live happily and to thrive.

GLOSSARY

habitat: the place where a plant or animal grows or lives

predator *(PRED-uh-tur)*: an animal that eats other animals for food

territory *(TARE-uh-tor-ree)*: an area *(AIR-ree-uh)* that is occupied *(AHK-yoo-pide)* or defended by an animal or groups of animals

skill: the ability to do something that comes from training, experience *(ex-PEER-ee-ens)*, and practice

bond: to form a close relationship

prance: to walk or move in a spirited *(SPEER-rih-ted)* manner

reed: a tall, thin grass that grows in wet areas

independent *(in-dee-PEN-dent)*: not relying on anyone or anything else

thistle *(THIS-ul)*: a wild plant that has sharp points on its leaves

QUESTIONS TO THINK ABOUT

1. Which of these three wild animals (hippos, tigers, and gorillas) do you think is the strongest, and how is it stronger than the others?

2. Some people might want to keep a wild animal as a pet. What are some reasons that it would NOT be a good idea to have any of these wild baby animals as a pet?

3. Playing is important to help learn and develop adult skills. What are some ways that tigers, hippos, and gorillas play? What skills are they developing?

4. In what ways are baby animals the same as baby humans? In what ways are they different?

Making Difficult Words Easy

Code Reader Books provide codes with "sound keys" to help read difficult words. For example, a word that may be challenging to read is "genius," so it might be followed by a code like this: genius *(JEEN-yus)*.

The codes use phonetic keys for each sound in the word. Knowing the keys can help make reading the codes easier.

Code Reader™ Keys

Long a sound (as in make):
a *(with a silent e)*, **ai**, or **ay**
Examples: break *(brake)*;
area *(AIR-ee-uh)*; able *(AY-bul)*

Short a sound (as in cat): **a**
Example: practice *(PRAK-tis)*

Long e sound (as in keep): **ee**
Example: complete *(kum-PLEET)*

Short e sound (as in set): **e** or **eh**
Examples: metric *(MEH-trik)*;
bread *(bred)*

Long i sound (as in by):
i *(with a silent e)* or **y**
Examples: might *(mite)*;
bicycle *(BY-sih-kul)*

Short i sound (as in sit): **i** or **ih**
Examples: myth *(mith)*;
condition *(kun-DIH-shun)*

Long u sound (as in cube): **yoo**
Example: unicorn *(YOO-nih-korn)*

Short u or schwa sound (as in cup):
u or **uh**
Examples: pension *(PEN-shun)*;
about *(uh-BOWT)*

Long o sound (as in hope):
o *(with a silent e)*, **oh**,
or **o** at the end of a syllable
Examples: molten *(MOLE-ten)*;
ocean *(OH-shen)*; nobody *(NO-bah-dee)*

Short o sound (as in top): **o** or **ah**
Examples: posture *(POS-chur)*;
bother *(BAH-ther)*

Long oo sound (as in cool): **oo**
Example: school *(skool)*

Short oo sound (as in look): **ŏŏ**
Examples: wood *(wŏŏd)*;
could *(kŏŏd)*

oy sound (as in boy): **oy**
Example: boisterous *(BOY-stur-us)*

ow sound (as in cow): **ow**
Example: discount *(DIS-kownt)*

aw sound (as in paw): **aw**
Example: faucet *(FAW-sit)*

qu sound (as in quit): **kw**
Example: question *(KWES-chun)*

zh sound (as in garage): **zh**
Example: fission *(FIH-zhun)*